Dear Reader,

On behalf of myself and the other contributing authors, I would like to welcome you to the seventh Open Door series. We hope that you enjoy the books and that reading becomes a lasting pleasure in your life.

Warmest wishes,

Patricia Scanlan.

Patricia Scanlan
Series Editor

THE OPEN DOOR SERIES IS DEVELOPED WITH THE ASSISTANCE OF THE CITY OF DUBLIN VOCATIONAL EDUCATION COMMITTEE.

Contents

My Difficult Childhood

I have never actually met anybody called Valentine. I suspect there is a bloody good reason for this. Calling one's child after one of the more obscure saints I can actually understand. But calling one's child Valentine would bring back wistful memories to most people. What does Valentine's Day really mean? I'm thinking of the canter down to the letterbox on the morning of February 14th. The blood scuttling through the veins at top speed. The tongue flapping with anticipation. The nerves doing cartwheels.

The agony of it all. Only to be followed by disappointment. The bare doormat. The cardless climb back up to the scratcher. The placing of the head beneath the blankets. The moistening of the pillow with tears so salty you could sprinkle them on chips. Calling one's child Valentine would be like calling it Disappointment. Disappointment O'Connor would not be much of a name for a child. No doubt, it would eventually get abbreviated to Dizzy O'Connor. I've met one or two of those in my time, God only knows. Sappy O'Connor would be another possibility, I suppose.

Anyway, of all the foul festive frolics, is there anything really worse than Saint Valentine's Day? The greeting-card hucksters need a little extra just to keep them in the style to which they are accustomed. Let us face it; desire is the most marketable concept there is.

When I was six I had a teacher called Miss Glennon. She was a very good teacher.

She believed that there was more to early education than the repetitive chanting of suspect nursery rhymes. When Saint Valentine's Day came around one year, she made every boy and girl in the class write a Valentine card, complete with a poem. For those less creative students, Miss Glennon explained that it was acceptable to start off with the time-honoured couplet 'roses are red, violets are blue'. We got ten minutes. The completed cards were then placed in two piles at the top of the class, one for boys and one for girls. We each had to pick one at random, and read it aloud to the assembled unwashed.

At the time, I entertained an uneasy but quite fervent affection for Michele Killen, a redhead who could play conkers like nobody's business, and whose pipe-cleaner men were the talk of the school. Michele did not like me much. On one occasion she called me "a weird little fecker", I recall. But, hey, it was kind of a Burton and Taylor thing. The card I picked out, however, came from a girl called Sheena, whose hand I always had to hold whenever Miss Glennon took us on nature walks. This was a little too often for my liking.

Flushed with romantic excitement, I stood up at the top of the class that morning long ago and began to read out the words Sheena had written. They were, and here I quote in full, "Roses are red, Violets are blue, I think you're horrible and you are like a poo." I was shattered. Not only was the thought less than affectionate, but it didn't even bloody scan properly.

Every time I think about it, I blush to the colour of Ribena. Saint Valentine has an awful lot to answer for, in my book. In the unlikely event of my ever making it into paradise, be assured I will certainly have a thing or two to say to him.

Another person from my difficult childhood I would like to meet, either in this life or the hereafter, is the famous and talented Australian entertainer, Mr Rolf Harris. You know, I actually used to like him a lot. When I was a nipper, the words of "Tie Me Kangaroo Down Sport" were as important to me as the words of the "Hail Holy Queen" were to other children.

I remember seeing his supreme Rolfness on *The Late Late Show* when I was a youngster. I think it was 1975. People had been on the show talking about Northern Ireland, about their lives and their sufferings, and about the deaths of their loved ones. Rolf Harris had been listening to all of this in the wings. He had been so moved that when he came on to perform he broke down in tears. It was an extraordinary sight, to a child. Rolf Harris simply stopped miming. He took off his glasses and put his hands to his face and cried, while the tape of his disembodied voice singing "Two Little Boys" continued to echo through the studio. It was one of the most important moments of my difficult childhood.

Yes, I had a spot in my heart for Rolf Harris. But he has burnt his boats with me now. In 1993 he released a cover version of Led Zeppelin's song "Stairway to Heaven". It got to number nine in the charts, which is argument, if such were needed, that young people today are only rabble and scum. Anyway, if I ever get my mitts on him, Rolf Harris will certainly be crying again.

You see, "Stairway to Heaven" is more than a song to me. The first girl who ever broke my heart did so while "Stairway to Heaven" was playing in the background. I was a mere boy, and I was in the Connemara Gaeltacht one summer. She was a little older than me, and she was reputed to know how to kiss people. When she kissed me, I became a little over-enthusiastic and my tongue got stuck in her braces. It was agonisingly painful. It took me ten whole minutes to free myself. My eyes still moisten, in fact, whenever I hear Irish spoken. Sometimes people misinterpret this as national pride.

She was from Baldoyle and I was from Glenageary. These delightful Dublin suburbs are separated by a distance of perhaps a dozen miles. But a dozen miles is practically an ocean when you're only a dozen years old. Anyway, immediately following her return to Baldoyle, the heartless little Jezebel seemed suddenly to remember that she had to play handball on a Wednesday after school. Now *there's* a thought-provoking excuse. This was the very afternoon we had set aside for our secret and passionate dates. She tried to let me down gently, but it was clear that the magic had just died. "Stairway to Heaven" came on as she gave me the big E. When the almost Yeatsian observation *"woarghh-oh, coz you know sometimes words have two meanings, unghg"* rang out of the jukebox, I told her I would never get over her. (By the way, if she's reading this now, I was lying.)

But ah, that delicately descending A-minor chord sequence with the bass part slithering down to F. Then soaring with the grace of a young albatross back up to the final G, A minor. Every two-bit guitarist in the world can play it. It's banned in some guitar shops, because people play it so much.

It used to be the last song of the night at the Presentation College disco, Glasthule, where I first strutted my funky stuff. "Prez", as it was known, was a pretty rough joint. They searched you outside for strong drink and offensive weapons. If you didn't have any, they didn't let you in. But "Stairway to Heaven" reduced even the most hardened gurriers, savage boot boys and ne'er-do-wells to wide-eyed blubbing wrecks. I can still see it now; a great head-banging mass of denim and cheesecloth and existential angst.

You know the bit where Robert Plant wails *"woooohooooh, and it makes me wonder, woooh yeah"*? I mean, you can keep your Seamus Heaneys; *that's* deep. And what does Rolf Harris do? The heartless reprobate "sings" this line. *"Wooooh-oooh, and it makes me wonder*". Then he quips, presumably to his backing group, "and how does it affect you blokes?" It's blasphemy. It's like spitting in the face of the *Mona Lisa*. When the time of retribution comes, this backing group needn't bother whimpering to me that they were only obeying orders.

And the brilliant bit at the end? You know the bit that goes BLAM BLAM, *CHUNK*, BLAM BLAM, *CHUNK*, BLAM A BLAM A BLAM A BLAM A *CHUNK CHUNK? And as we wind on down the road…* Only the crowning glory, I mean the musical equivalent of the Sistine bloody Chapel ceiling, and Rolf leaves it out! God, it's like saying the Mass without bothering to have the consecration. It's pointless.

This is surely the worst period ever for popular music. When I was a teenager, people were embarrassed about liking Slade, The Sweet, Mudd and Alvin Stardust. These days, Alvin's "Won't You Be My Coo Ca Choo" seems like a Bach prelude and

Mudd's "Tiger Feet" has all the brooding sexual magnetism of early Elvis. The charts are full of trite cover versions, and rich kiddies chanting about machine guns and the size of their penises over dull synthesizer beats. Me, I'm pining for Horslips. I'm missing Thin Lizzy. This is my past that Rolf Harris and his hell-spawned ilk are messing with. Hold me down, boys, till I strap on my air guitar. Rolf Harris, I'm coming after you, sucker. In my dreams, you are forever in the playground of Saint Joseph of Cluny School, Glenageary, and I am there too, giving you an eternal dead leg.

But dreams work strangely. One minute you are in Casablanca with Cindy Crawford, the next you are in Castlepollard with Michael Crawford. You never know what is going to happen in a dream. You never know what's going to happen in real life either, but some things you can be relatively confident about. The truth will always hurt, half your socks will always disappear in the washing machine and John Bruton in full flight will always be strangely reminiscent of Kermit the Frog in *The Muppet Show*.

One night recently I had a strange dream, one which I've had many times before. In this dream I am seventeen. My face is a sordid mess of oozing carbuncles and leaking pustules. I am about to do my Leaving Certificate maths exam. The *cigire*, a tall ungainly fellow with wings and a large yellow beak, is flapping up and down the aisle. Another teacher is sitting at the desk next to mine, laughing at me. I should explain that this dreamlike teacher is, or more accurately was, a real teacher, a kind-hearted priest who taught me once and has now passed on to what I hope will be a pleasant reward. If he's up there now I expect he's got the Jacuzzi, because Janey Mack, does he deserve it.

This poor holy man had been on the missions in Africa, and had gotten a chunk chawed out of him by some insect. To recuperate, he had been sent home to Ireland to teach teenage boys. Wonderful, huh? Rampant malaria must have seemed almost cuddly compared to the suffering we put him through. Truly, we made his life such agony that he must have often wished he was back on the banks of the Zambezi taking his chances with whatever beastie might next come cantering out of the jungle. He was a thick-haired cove when he began to instruct us in second year. By the time we got to the Leaving Cert he was a basket case, bald as a snooker ball. He was thus given the affectionate nickname "Penis Head". In the end, I think that's what drove him over the edge. I used to imagine him looking at himself in the mirror while shaving every morning and hoarsely whispering, "I don't really look like that, do I? I don't. No, I don't. I *couldn't*."

Anyway, back to this dream. There I am in the hall, with poor old PH (RIP) munching his fingernails and mumbling about the Zulus. I turn over the maths exam paper and begin to read. With cold horror, I realise that I cannot answer any of the questions. I have to sit and watch everyone else write. It is horrible. So horrible, indeed, that I always like having this dream, because it is so incredibly pleasant to wake up from.

My Leaving Certificate maths exam has haunted my nights for the last thirteen years. I was always desperate at maths. I could never understand it. Teenage life seemed so full of real problems that inventing ones in order to solve them seemed absurd. Why was it important to know how quickly a half-full train doing average speed would get to Limerick Junction via Portarlington when I could spend my days dreaming up witty things to murmur during the slow sets at Prez? ("Listen, Concepta, can I buy you a fizzy orange after 'Freebird' or would you rather just have the money?") Even now, I only remember one mathematical fact. The square on the hypotenuse equals the sum of

the squares of the other two sides. The
other two sides of *what*, I never knew.
(Smoked salmon, is it?)

Each and every June, Ireland is full of
stressed young people worrying about
exams. They are important, of course, but
one thing should be made clear. Exams
examine your ability to do exams. They have
nothing at all to do with education. They're
not worth going bananas over. "If God
must test us," Woody Allen quipped, "I wish
he'd give us a written." But God, if he exists,
and if he is testing us at all, is doing so by
continuous assessment. There will not be a
cigire on the last day of judgement. No way.
So what I want to know is this: if it's good
enough for God, then, why, damn it all, *why*
couldn't it have been good enough for the
civil service?

Anyway, in time, my difficult childhood
ended. I grew up and out, and I started
going to pop concerts. It was a decision I
was often to regret. What is this tragic

madness that takes hold of the youth of Ireland? It is still beyond my understanding that every summer in our country young people trek off to Slane or some other sad little town to git on up, shake their booties, sink ankle deep into country muck and consume dubious hamburgers, some of which have prices as artificially pumped up as the cows from which they once came.

In the entire line-up of cultural tortures, is there anything really worse than the outdoor rock festival? I mean, yours truly is no party pooper. Be assured, yours truly has gotten down with the best of them, put my funk in many faces and agreed, quite fervently, that boogie nights are always the best in town. My own bootie has been shaken as thoroughly as James Bond's martini. But I draw the line at the rock festival. If there is a hell being prepared for me somewhere – and I feel sure there is – it is an eternity of Lord Henry Mountcharles and his famous back garden.

I spent my teenage years going to rock festivals. I have seen the horror. I know what gives. You go down the country on a rattling coach, suffering from an appalling hangover. When you arrive in Slane/Thurles/Tramore, you realise that the locals have discovered the fine art of fleecing Van Morrison fans instead of sheep. You mortgage your as-yet-unborn first child to pay for a Coca Cola and begin the three-mile trek over rough country to get to the venue. It is your luck to come across one of those festering demons who pose as security staff. By the time you are granted admission, Sting is on stage, saying that we all godda, y'know, do a liddle bit more for the environment and animal rights. You feel you would be quite happy not to buy shoes made of animal skin, if only you could buy shoes made of *Sting*'s skin. You just want to go home and back to bed, but you can't, because you're *having a good time*.

As Prince says in one of his songs, "Dig, if you will, the picture." There are seventy thousand punters all being whipped into a quite advanced and dangerous state of sexual excitement by the throbbing primitive beat. All of them are very much the worse for strong drink. Thirty-five thousand of them are sitting on the shoulders of the other thirty-five thousand, waving cameras and plastic bottles of hooch in the air. The place is crawling with lost and screeching infants, savage dogs, arguing couples, plain-clothes members of the drug squad, stoned ravers in psychedelic shirts, Fine Gael TDs and recently released political prisoners trying to get their photographs into the newspapers. Neil Young is on the stage now, yowling and wailing and falling about and thrashing his tuneless guitar – "*I wanna live, I wanna give, I've been a miner for a heart of gold.*" The hippies think this is deep and people are trying to dance to this. In truth you couldn't even do your shopping to it. All around the edges of this vast and restless crowd, people are queuing up to evacuate their bowels in the nettle bushes. You can't face this, so you go back, and you try to find your friends, but it's impossible. It's getting terrifically hot now, and The Saw Doctors come on and everyone jumps up and down and roars and someone tramples on your toes. There are long lines of punk rockers all puking and fighting and interfering with each other. There are sunstroke victims having visions of the Blessed Virgin Mary. There are Chris de Burgh fans having terrible fits, insanely screaming the words of "Patricia The Stripper". There are young fainting women being passed over the heads of the fevered crowd. There are bottles of lager being passed through the crowd too, and parched punters down the back are gratefully swigging. What they don't realise is that the diehards up the front have finished their homebrew. Not wanting to lose their places in the throng, they have put those plastic bottles to a use that nature never intended, then turned and flung them into the sea of bodies. Your nose starts to bleed with tension, all over your shirt, and you look like the victim of a gang attack. One more fat once-relevant pop star in unwise trousers bounds out on stage and bellows, "YEAH, WOAH, yeah, all RIGHT, SLANE! You're BEAUTIFUL! HOW YA DOIN'? I CAN'T HEAR YOU! Rock and ROLL, ALL RIGHT!" You stop and realise that you may be young, but you're already pining for the time you can stay in of a summer afternoon and lie on the couch with a large gin and tonic and watch the bloody television, instead of going to rock concerts.

Of course, you have to be careful about relaxing too. It can be a very dangerous activity. One afternoon recently, I actually tried to do this. Relax, I mean. I wandered casually over to my parents' house with the intention of spending a few pleasant hours with my loving brothers and sisters. An hour later, to drown out the noise of the roaring, I turned on the radio. A man from the

Labour Party was on, talking about emigration and our young people.

He was in generous mood. He had no problem at all with the emigrants being given the vote, he said. I thought this was big of him, considering that the disastrous policies of the last Labour–Fine Gael government are what has most of them emigrants in the first place. Ah, the memories of my university days came flooding back.

The very socialist and progressive Labour Party was in government when I was in my second year in university. One of the really progressive things it wanted to do was to take the medical card away from students. OK, so I know that's not exactly the bombing of Guernica, but, hey, we were upset about it at the time. We were young, I suppose.

We all met in Trinity College. There was going to be an occupation. Our student union leader told us to be low-key. Fifty of us took our bus fares, our banners and our bullhorns and we marched down to the Department of Health looking about as low-key as the massed Serbian irregulars on a day trip to a mosque.

Once we had penetrated the minister's office, we all sat down on the shag pile and waited for something revolutionary to happen. I had taken along my cigarette lighter so that if anyone struck up a sudden chorus of "We Shall Not Be Moved" or "Blowing in the Wind", I could hold it up in the air and wave it meaningfully from side to side. I was very optimistic in those days.

After a while the police arrived. They were quite angry. They said they would "do whatever was necessary" to get us out. They repeated the phrase a few times. We scoffed, heroically. We'd be here, we said, until all of our demands had been met. They asked what these demands were. There seemed to be a bit of confusion at this point. Personally, in addition to having Ireland immediately declared a 32-county socialist republic, I wanted to have a regular girlfriend and *Brideshead Revisited* repeated on a Monday night. Anyway, while we argued, the coppers left, no doubt happily reflecting on the fact that their monthly PAYE payments were helping to subsidise our youthful exuberance.

Their sergeant came in then, a nice big fellow from Cork. He parked his ample behind on the minister's desk. He told us that we were all very bright young people (which, incidentally, was questionable in a number of cases). He said we were very lucky to be getting an education (which, incidentally, was true). Then he asked us to leave. We told him to shag away off to hell, him and his fascist free-state, goose-stepping, imperialist paymasters. Well actually, I think we just said no. He shook his head sadly. He took off his cap. It was a terrifying sight, for some reason, a policeman taking off his cap.

OK, he sighed, there was one thing he wanted to say, before giving the order for us to be forcibly removed. The phrases "give the order" and "forcibly removed" were quite effective, now that I think of it. You could almost hear the sound of fifty pairs of buttocks being clenched with anxiety at the same time.

He pointed a finger. "If any of you are arrested today," he breathed, "you'll get a criminal record." We greeted this threat with jeers and coarse whistles. "And if you get a criminal record," he continued, "you will never get into America." There followed a silence which can only be described as stunned. "Never," he said. "Never. Think it over." He told us he would give us ten minutes to consider our options. He slipped from the room like a graceful phantom.

Reader, no water cannon was ever so effective. There was a stampede out of that office. There was dust coming out of the carpet. It was like the back door of a brothel during a raid.

I hung on with the hard core. At the time, I was going through that stage of adolescence known as virulent anti-Americanism, so I didn't really care what would happen. What did happen was that two hefty guards carried me out and dumped me down on the steps so hard that I nearly shattered my spine. It was ten years ago. I've put on a bit of weight since. It would take the whole cast of *Hill Street Blues* to do the same job now.

Anyway, that sergeant understood something very important. He understood that our politicians are such embarrassing, dismal failures that emigration is an utterly ingrained part of the Irish psyche. Growing up in Dublin, you just expect emigration to happen to you, like puberty. In Chile the cops attach electrodes to your private parts. In Ireland they just tell you you'll never be able to emigrate. It works too. It's the biggest threat of them all.

The Birds and the Bees:
How to Fall in Love

Even before my difficult childhood had
ended, I already knew that the most
important thing I would learn in school was
that almost everything I would learn in
school would be useless. When I was fifteen
I knew the principal industries of the Ruhr
Valley, the underlying causes of World War
One and what Peig Sayers had for her dinner
every day. Did even one minuscule titbit
from this assortment of knowledge ever
come in handy in later life? Did it my
buttocks. What I wanted to know when I

was fifteen was the best way to chat up girls. That is what I still want to know.

It's something I have never been able to do. I have "friends" who know how to do it and I loathe them with an almost religious intensity. You know the type. Relaxed, easy manner, cheekbones you could hang a hat on. Normal, well-adjusted men who've had their teeth capped, read three of the novels on the Booker Prize short list and once been to an opera directed by Jonathan bloody Miller. Vile unspeakable pond scum, in other words, but boy do they know how to get on – and indeed off – with women.

Last summer I was in New York, reading a copy of *The Village Voice* one day, when my eyes fell upon an advertisement for flirting classes. "Huh," I thought, "I don't care if I can't chat anyone up. Only a *really* sad person would ever do something as incredibly stupid as a flirting class."

On the first night I was ten minutes late. By the time I arrived there were six men and seven women, all of them fidgeting, blushing, biting their fingernails, gnawing their lips. All of them hoping too that by the end of the evening the lips they would be gnawing would be firmly attached to the face of somebody else. It was a hot Manhattan night and the sexual tension in that classroom was sparking. The air seemed drenched with pheromones. If you had inhaled suddenly you would have got pregnant with quads.

The teacher breezed into the room like a pop star arriving backstage at Wembley. Her name was Lucy. She was a wonderful gal, a vision in stretch Lycra and black 501s. She made us feel that it was OK not to know how to flirt. It didn't necessarily mean that we weren't attractive (I have to say, I wasn't too crazy about that "necessarily"), but it was an important skill to acquire. Most relationships, after all, began with a flirtation. My own usually began with an act of emotional hara-kiri, I reflected, but that was another story.

Lucy kicked off with a bit of guff on feeling good about ourselves in social situations. Dinner parties, for example. I ignored this. Dinner parties, after all, are not there to make us feel good about ourselves. Dinner parties are there to remind us that God does exist and that he hates us. If we were the kind of people who felt good about ourselves at dinner parties, then why the fuck weren't we at one? Why were we forking out good hard-earned cash to sit in a stuffy classroom reeking of sexual panic and trying to look like we were only here because we wanted to write an article?

Things improved when we got down to the specifics. *Step one: Basic Flirtation.* Lucy said you had to look the desired person in the eye. You had to smile and use the person's name. You had to pay compliments and, if at all possible, touch the person. Not run your mitts all over them, of course, just "lightly brush" against them, preferably while "sharing a joke". A joke came thundering into my mind. What's the difference between a raw egg and a good ride? You can beat a raw egg. Perhaps that was not the kind of joke you would share with a total stranger. Above all, Lucy said, you had to ask questions. So far so good, I felt. I like asking people questions; it is a very good way to stop people asking questions about you.

Next stage was *Getting That Date*. Lucy said she would give us her secret weapon. The hormonal activity in the room seemed suddenly to surge. She leaned forward. "Little pauses," Lucy whispered.

Basically, the gist was that we were not supposed to go blundering in, grinning, "Howarya petal? Fancy a tequila sunrise or what?" We were supposed to "insert a little pause".

Lucy showed us what she meant. I was selected as guinea pig. She came over, sat down and gazed into my face, touching my wrist with just the right degree of pressure.

My God, if there was one thing this woman understood, it was gravitational pull. She smiled. She moved her hair gently away from her sparkling eyes. She was so close that I could smell her musky perfume. The class inhaled, *en masse*. I felt my palms moisten.

"Listen, Joe," she beamed. "Do you, uh, want to have a drink with me sometime?"

The class exhaled and almost burst into applause. "Are turkeys fucking nervous in November, Lucy?" I thought, silently. "I see what you mean," I said.

"Now you try it," she grinned.

We broke into pairs and I got Alison, a very nice legal secretary from the Bronx. I noticed that on the name badge she was wearing she had drawn a little smiley face where the dot over the "i" in her name should have been. That apart, things were looking up. "Now," Lucy said, in the cool tone of voice used by brain surgeons who are just about to go into someone's brain with a revved-up Black and Decker, "Look into the eyes." I peered into Alison's pupils as though she were Dan Quayle and I was trying to find measurable evidence of human life.

"OK, people," Lucy urged. "Now smile, speak, and *insert that pause.*"

I could feel the sweat trickling down my back. "Emmm," I grinned. "You, uh, want to have a drink with me sometime?"

Alison laughed so hard that a ball of snot came shooting out of her nose with the force of a missile. I wondered whether this was my opportunity to "brush lightly" against her by offering her a tissue, or, at the very least, the back of my sleeve.

"Use Alison's name, Joe," Lucy chuckled, throatily. "You've inserted, but you haven't used her name yet." I conceded that this had indeed been an error of some magnitude.

I tried again. "Urgh, Alison, you, um, want to have a drink some time, hrnmgh?" The entire class collapsed into a frenzy of tittering. It was dreadful. You could have eliminated the national debt of a small third-world country with the amount of money these people had spent on psychotherapy. Yet here they were; control freaks, social inadequates and tragic misfits all, weeping tears of laughter, slapping not only their own thighs but each other's also. It was very unfair, I felt.

I attempted it once more. "Urff, Alison, I dunno, you hmmmm, wanna go…?" People were practically on the floor now. Bill, a very pleasant chap from Queens, had to get up and leave the room, shaking uncontrollably, hankie clasped to his frantically guffawing gob. I just couldn't figure it out. Every time I asked Alison if she wanted to have a drink, I sounded as if I was already pissed. It was a hopeless situation. My little pauses were yawning chasms of existential angst.

Outside, later, fourteen of us stood on the sidewalk. We all agreed, quite dishonestly in my view, that it had been "a lot of fun", but that some of us would have to work harder than others. We said our goodbyes and went to leave. I walked a block with Alison and Bill in nervous silence. Then, very suddenly, Bill stopped and slapped himself on the forehead, as though swatting some particularly virulent breed of mosquito.

"Urm, Alison?" he said. "Hey, I just thought, I'm like, going uptown. You, er, wanna share a taxi?"

She turned, the pale pink haze of the streetlight caressing the side of her angelic face. She reached out and touched his wrist. "Uh, yeah, Bill," she smiled. "Yeah. That'd be really neat."

"Errmm?" I ejaculated, hopefully, "urrfmfgh?" But, tragically, too late. The taxi pulled up and, in an instant, they were gone.

And as I stood on the pavement alone, watching their yellow cab roar off into the sultry heat of the Manhattan night, I couldn't help but reflect that when dealing with women, it is a truly wonderful thing to have had an education.

This was a thought that had occurred to me many times before, of course, particularly in my student days. I should explain that in my home town of Dublin, in the grounds of Trinity College, a near-legendary event called the Trinity Ball is held every year. Although officially only open to students at that marvellously appointed inner-city university, it is actually attended by large numbers of students from other establishments, including my own fair and glorious alma mater, University College Dublin.

Anyway, the Trinity Ball begins at midnight and ends with a huge outdoor disco at dawn the following morning. During this time, attending students are expected to get togged up in formal gear, get drunk and get stoned. Perhaps most importantly, they are expected to get off vigorously with the person they came with, or, failing that, whoever else they can lay their hands on. Well, hey, it didn't actually say that on the tickets, but that was certainly my understanding. It was, without a doubt, the worst evening of my entire life.

The woman I went with was a lithe creature with blonde hair, a stunning smile and legs that seemed to go all the way up to her armpits. When I tell you that she had something of the startled deer about her, I do not mean that she had antlers. Rather, her eyes, when she turned suddenly to look at you, were just mesmerisingly cute. She was a stunner. She was the princess of Babelonia. I could easily have consumed a large portion of *pommes frites* out of her intimate undergarments.

I was highly surprised that she had agreed to go with me to the ball, because I knew that I was not at all her type. She tended to bestow her favours on aspiring rock stars, Keanu Reeves look-alikes, men with silky skin and broad shoulders and a total lack of musical talent. I don't know now why I asked her, but somehow I did. To my astonishment she agreed.

However, at the pre-ball party which our mutual friends had thrown, I began to realise that the evening was not going to end in the shattering banquet of mutual carnal fulfilment that I had had in mind. It was the small things really. The look of cold horror that came over her face when she saw my hired evening suit; its stained lapels flapping like the wings of a deranged angel. The way she vomited up her twiglets with the force of a broken-down fruit machine when I tried to hold her hand in the kitchen. I dealt with my teenage nervousness by drinking an entire bowl of rum punch, smoking several joints and trying to snog somebody else upstairs in the toilet.

I was very drunk by the time the fleet of taxis arrived to convey us all into town, and, for some reason, my date did not seem to want to sit beside me. In fact, it was only with considerable effort that I managed to dissuade her from strapping herself to the roof-rack, or following us in on the bus.

We stood in the queue outside Trinity for half an hour, during which time we did not exchange one single word. Well, I think I tried out my favourite joke. Once upon a time there were three bears. Now there's bloody millions of them. Astonishingly, she didn't even titter. Once in, I got even more drunk and I fell asleep on the floor of the Examination Hall. As I recall, The Pogues were playing; a difficult band to fall asleep to. When I woke up, my head was hammering, my left shoe *and* sock were missing and there was a large muddy footprint on the front of my tuxedo. For some reason I have never been able to figure out, my date was gone. I searched the room, elbowing my way through the perspiring swarm of diddley-eying Trinity students, but she was nowhere to be seen.

I sought her out in the bar and the restaurant, on the rugby pitch and in the Arts Block. I got the security men to broadcast a message over the intercom. I lurched up and down the quad, trying to describe her to total strangers. Most of them laughed, jeered or pelted me with water-inflated condoms. One of them tried to piss on me. Unmentionable rustlings were going on in the bushes, where the spirit of Saint Valentine was being commemorated *al fresco*. Such was my total stupidity, my drunkenness and immaturity, that I actually managed to persuade myself it had all been a *mis-understanding*. My love would fall into my arms just the moment I found her, before leading me gratefully into the shrubbery by my dickey-bow. Oh, the terrible thing that is young male self-delusion. I bellowed out her name like a foghorn, or a snog-horn. But no trace of my punk-rock Cinderella.

I finally caught up with her at the dawn disco, at seven thirty in the morning. It was very cold, a light rain was falling, and she was snogging the gob off my best friend's brother. She had her hand up the back of his shirt, I noticed. Had she been sucking his

THE SHORTER IRISH MALE

face any harder his skin would have simply peeled away in her mouth. I turned around and hopped all the way home, where I collapsed on my bed, took off my tuxedo, lit my last cigarette and cried myself into oblivion.

Fun, I think it is called. I remember my kind and gentle stepmother consoling me at the time, saying that relationships become easier the older you get. Little did I know how spectacularly untrue that was. Love is never easy. Getting into it is almost impossible and getting out of it is even harder. I remember once having a relationship with this crazed woman who really didn't like me very much. Things were kind of tense between us. In fact, things got so tense that it often felt that our relationship was being directed by Alfred Hitchcock.

I had cause to reflect on all this recently, while having dinner with a close woman friend. It was one of those upmarket restaurants where the waiter insists that you call him Serge, when, really, you would much rather call him waiter. And the subject turned, as for some reason it often does when you eat polenta, to love.

This woman is going out with a prize bozo, who possesses the brains of a piece of toast, the charm of Margaret Thatcher and the looks of Rod Steiger. He is an aspiring actor, actually. His performances are not so much wooden as finest mahogany. "I haven't got the guts to finish with him," my friend said to me. "I'll break his heart." I sat there nodding sympathetically, hoovering up lengths of spaghetti into my gob as discreetly as possible. I was thinking that it wasn't dreamboat's heart that needed breaking, so much as his coccyx. Suddenly, a very simple solution occurred to me. "I'll do it," I said. "I'll finish it for you."

I am now prepared to extend this new service to the readers of this book. "AN IRISH MALE DUMP-THE-CHUMP

PROMOTION!" Here's how it works. You send me your hard-earned cash, and I do your dirty work for you. Simple or what? For ten pounds plus VAT you get the basic service. I ring up the mistreating brain-dead sap you used to be sad enough to snog. I tell them they can shag away off and die because you are fed up wandering about with WELCOME on your back. You don't want them anymore. Furthermore, you never *did* really want them. If the survival of the entire human race depended on you having sex with them just one last time, for about thirty seconds, and for a billion pounds, you would say no, you scum-sucking sweaty-buttocked foul-breathed bandy-legged bollocks.

For thirty pounds, we can go a little up-market. I will turn up on their doorstep masquerading as an elder of the Mormon church. I will invite myself in for coffee, and say, "Listen, _____ (your name here) really does like you a lot, an *awful* lot, straight up, but he/she just doesn't like you *in that special way.*" I will then dry their weeping eyes with a Kleenex, wipe their nose on my newly laundered sleeve and tell them not to worry about it. While there may not be too many more fish in the sea, post-Sellafield, there are certainly plenty more poison-spitting snakes in the cesspit.

After that, it does start to get a bit pricey. But worth it. Spare yourself all the guilt, the recrimination, the tears and accusations. Spare yourself the ripped-up lovey-dovey photographs of you and your formerly better half sharing cocktails on a balcony somewhere, returned to you in a re-useable envelope with the word "bastard" inserted between your first name and your second. Avoid the cute little fluffy toy rabbit wearing the "Gee, I weally wuv you cos you're such a cuddlesome funny bunny" T-shirt that you gave her/him last Valentine's Day being anonymously delivered back to your place of work in a shoebox with a stake through its heart. It's simple. You just pay me, and I take the rap.

There are several optional extras of course. For twenty pounds, I am prepared to say you have some infectious venereal disease that will surely rot the very fundament off anyone misfortunate enough to come within a donkey's bray of you. For thirty, I will tell them you are a Spurs supporter or a secret born-again Christian. For fifty, I will say you once owned a copy of "Shang-a-Lang" by The Bay City Rollers.

I will, however, have to ask for danger money if you expect me to use corny lines. You're just not good enough for them? A tenner surtax. You're coming out of quite a long relationship in which you were deeply hurt and you're just, you know, not ready for that kind of serious commitment yet? Twenty. You don't really know what's wrong, but it's all down to your difficult childhood and the fact that you didn't get enough hugs from your parents? A particular favourite of my own, I must say. Thirty-five. And then there's the deluxe service.

For one hundred and ninety-five pounds, I will take your partner out to supper in a fancy joint, ply them with veal's throats, pheasant's tongues and vintage champagne. I will flirt like Zsa Zsa Gabor and discourse at length on W. H. Auden (or any major twentieth-century poet of your choice – January is a special Pablo Neruda month). I will make them feel great about themselves, tell them how beautiful and intelligent they are. Even – perhaps *especially* – if they are stupid and ugly enough to turn water sour. Let's face it, they probably are; otherwise you wouldn't be in need of this service. I will cackle at their terrible jokes, then slowly bring the subject around to *you*. I will explain with tenderness and sensitivity that, hey, it's so *so* tragic, but the magic just slipped right away while you weren't looking. Still, I shall say, it was a beautiful thing while it lasted. I'll say that you feel you're not so much closing a door on your love as sealing a perfectly wonderful memory in the emotional aspic of the past. The hankies with which I will mop your now ex-beloved's tears will be of finest hand-spun silk. The shoulders of my jacket, into which the broken-hearted dumpee may plunge her or his wailing and snivelling chops, will be efficiently padded. The songs I gently croon as I take hold of your trashed darling-no-more's screeching face and slap, *slap*, slap again to calm them down will be purest Manilow. Go on. Christmas is coming. You know it makes sense. Dump that chump.

It's not that I want to be cynical. If you have met the right person, you should do the right thing, and marry them immediately. In fact, two good friends of mine who have been going out together – and, worse, God help us all, quite frequently staying in together and refusing to answer the telephone – told their families recently that they were going to get married soon.

(Happily enough, to each other.) I was pleased to hear this news, because I am a great believer in the institution of marriage, and I can hardly wait to get married myself. In fact, I intend to do so as often as possible. Not that I am a romantic or anything. It is just that if I am going to get fat, disillusioned and sad, I am bloody well taking somebody with me.

We talked for a while about their impending nuptials, my friends and myself. I am to be a witness on the happy occasion. I dislike the word witness, really, for its unpleasant legal overtones. I mean, you could just as easily be a witness at somebody's divorce as their marriage. And am I to be a witness for the prosecution or the defence? I think I should be told.

I am to make a speech on the day, and I was instructed by the bride-to-be not to use the words "wedding" or "marriage" in this speech. We finally settled on the "bonding", which phrase I am not particularly happy about. I feel it conjures up agonising and highly embarrassing scenes involving super-glue, crowbars, teams of strong men and large tubs of axle grease. But who am I to disappoint a blushing bride? Bonding it is.

Marriage has not been very fashionable in ultra-liberal circles for some time. I lived in London for some years. In certain parts of that right-on, politically correct city, if you happened to let slip at a dinner party that you were thinking of getting married, people peered at you as though you had just farted during the funeral of a prominent member of the ANC. There then ensued a turgid lecture from some poloneck-wearing part-time poet about just how conventional and middle-class marriage was, immediately before the hostess brought in the desiccated kiwi fruit for dessert.

I cannot figure out why marriage has such a bad press. It is a romantic and idealistic institution, but surely we need more romance in this lonely world. Yes, I know some marriages sadly do not work out. But governments do not work out either, from time to time, and we do not pooh-pooh the general idea of democracy as a result. And yes, on paper, marriage makes very little sense. How in the name of God are you supposed to find the one person you can love for the rest of your life, and go on loving them and putting up with their weird antics, cranky opinions and off-putting personal habits? How are you supposed to cleave to this one special soul mate, even in the event that some balmy night, just after you have enjoyed frenzied connubial congress, she may sigh deeply, light up a fag, rest her head on your breast and confide that she feels Daniel O'Donnell isn't actually *that* bad, y'know, if you really listen to the words of "Whatever Happened to Old Fashioned Love"?

The idea that marriage provides security is incorrect. But insecurity is the whole point of matrimony. You may think you are certain of your feelings, yet marriage at its most essential is the emotional equivalent of jumping out of an airplane not knowing whether the bundle so firmly strapped to your back contains a parachute or a grand piano. I've never been spliced myself, but I can understand how some folks find it more exciting to plummet through mid-air thinking "so far, so good" than to sit in the cockpit, fly the plane and admire the scenery below.

Not that I'm necessarily recommending marriage for everybody. Different strokes, as the conservative MP exclaimed in the massage parlour. I spoke to another pal about the subject recently. The unhappy chap is knocking about with a woman who wants to marry him, but he does not share her desire. (In conversation, he often refers to his unfortunately intense beloved by the pseudonym Wanda, which, he says, stands for "What? Another Neurotic Disaster? Absolutely!" "It's awful," he sighed, "Wanda's gone and bought herself a year's sub-scription to *Bride To Be* Magazine." His face took on the length of a fortnight's holiday in Termonfeckin. "Well, look," I suggested, "her birthday's coming up. You could always extend it to five years as a present." He looked at me blankly, then. And for one awful moment, I felt sure he thought I was serious.

Banana Republic:
Recollections of a Suburban Irish Childhood

In the summer of 1977 I was thirteen years old and pretty miserable with my life. My parents' marriage – unhappy for a long time – had finally disintegrated in the most bitter circumstances. My father had moved out of the house. He had applied to the courts for custody of myself, my two sisters and my brother, and won his case. On the day he had come back to collect us and take us to our new home, I had asked him to let me stay living with my mother. I felt sorry for her, I suppose, and I did not want her to be left on her own. My father agreed that I could do this. He was very good about it.

We lived in a five-bedroomed house in Glenageary, a middle-class suburb of south-side Dublin. There was a large stain on the gable wall, which, if you glanced at it in a certain light, looked like the map of Ireland. I always thought that meant something important, but I could never figure out what exactly. My parents, both of whom came from working-class Dublin backgrounds, had slogged and scraped hard to buy this house, at a time when things must have seemed full of possibility for them. They must have had great plans for what they would do in that house. But in the summer of 1977, with only myself and my mother living there, the house seemed unutterably empty, haunted by lost expectations.

We fought a lot, my mother and I. She had wonderful qualities. She also had a passionate nature, which the circumstances of her life had somehow forced down a wrong turn, so that it had taken the shape of anger. She possessed a capacity for doing great harm to people she loved, and that must have made her very unhappy. When I think about her now, I try to do so with compassion and love. Like all unhappy people, she deserved that. But in those days, we hurt each other a lot, my mother and I. We didn't see eye to eye on *anything*. Sometimes she would throw me out of the house; other times I would simply walk out to get away from her. So what I'm saying is that I spent a good deal of the very hot summer of 1977 just wandering around the streets of Dublin by myself.

An odd thing was happening in Dublin in the summer of 1977. All of a sudden, a strange thing called punk rock had arrived in town. People were suddenly talking about it everywhere you went. Up and down Grafton Street, in the arcades of the

Dandelion Market on St Stephen's Green, in Freebird Records – a sleazily glamorous shop down on the quays of the River Liffey – the young people of my own age were all talking about it.

At first in Dublin, punk rock was nothing much more than a feeling. I mean, nobody *knew* very much about it. It was said that it had been started over in London the year before, by a group called the Sex Pistols, who swore at people during interviews and were generally controversial. But nobody I knew had much more knowledge than that. Punk had been initially perceived as just another English invention, I suppose, another weird Limey oddity, in the same culturally wacko league as eel pie, pantomime dames and The Good Old Days.

But that summer, posters for home-grown punk-rock groups – or, more accurately, groups that posed as punk groups – suddenly started to appear around Dublin. I remember starting to notice them, in places like the Coffee Inn on South Anne Street, where I used to go and sit for hours over a single Coca-Cola. Posters for The Atrix, The Blades, The Boyscoutz, Big Self, Berlin, The New Versions, Rocky de Valera and the Gravediggers, The Vultures, The Bogey Boys, The Virgin Prunes, The Radiators From Space. I may be wrong about some of these bands – I mean that I may have got their dates of birth wrong by a few months – but in my mind and memory, they all appeared in Dublin in the hot summer of 1977. I remember seeing the names of these new bands on these lurid posters, how exotic and mysterious the words seemed, how funny sometimes. There was a band called Free Booze, who had called themselves this because it was a good way to catch people's attention. And there was an odd little outfit of northside born-again Christians who played Peter Frampton songs, and who, it was said, would never amount to anything. In the summer of 1977, they were just about to change their name from The Hype to U2.

All these bands had sprung up more or less overnight in Dublin, it seemed to me. And at around the same time, a disc jockey called Dave Fanning, who worked on a pirate radio station called ARD, had started to play punk rock on his show. Also, a strange new music magazine called *Hot Press* had just started up, carrying regular articles about punk rock, reviews of records, news of punk-rock gigs. It was odd. But slowly, punk rock was starting to seep into Dublin. And in the summer after my brother and sisters went away to live with my dad, I spent many nights in my room listening to Dave Fanning, reading Bill Graham or Niall Stokes in *Hot Press*, avoiding my mother and wondering what to make of my life, and of punk rock.

It is important to say that this was a time when Dublin did not really exist on the world rock and roll map. We had Thin

Lizzy and Rory Gallagher and a Celtic rock band called Horslips, but that was about it. Foreign acts simply did not play in Ireland. It would have been almost unheard of for a big American or British band to gig in Dublin. The city had no pop culture of any size or significance. But in the summer of 1977, when I was thirteen, into this vacuum stepped a monstrous and slavering spirit.

Punk had a notion of secrecy about it in Ireland, a vague redolence of semi-illegality. Someone once told me that when Freebird Records first got in copies of the Sex Pistols record *Never Mind the Bollocks*, for instance, the customs officers had obliterated the word "Bollocks" with strips of red sellotape. And RTÉ, the national radio station, refused to play punk at all. "Punk rock is junk rock," announced Larry Gogan, then Ireland's foremost disc jockey. Punk felt kind of taboo. So to people of my age, it felt attractive.

I got a job that July, working as a tea boy on a building site in Dalkey, which was near where I lived with my mother. It was great to get out of the house, wonderful to have somewhere to go during the day. One of the labourers on the site was a tall scrawny fellow called Hubert. Hubert was about nineteen, I suppose, from the working-class suburb of Sallynoggin. His language was atrocious. He peppered his sentences with the word "fuck". Sometimes he would even insert it between the syllables of another word. One day, for instance, I heard him refer to his home town as "Sally-fuckin'-noggin".

Hubert had worked as a bus conductor for a time, before being dismissed in unknown circumstances and coming to lift blocks on the sites. There were two things that made his life complete. The first was pornography. He had a vast and com-prehensive collection of *Playboys* and *Penthouses*, which had been sent over every month for some years by his brother in England. (Such publications were not then legally available in Ireland.) Hubert would cut pictures out of these magazines and sell them individually to the other men on the site, thus garnering enormous profits. It was fifty pence for a picture that featured a pair of breasts, I remember, and seventy-five pence for what Hubert called "a gee". This was a word I had never heard before, a coarse Dublin euphemism for a vagina. "Seventy-fuckin'-five pence a gee-shot," he would sigh, shaking his head and refusing to haggle.

The second thing that made Hubert's life complete was punk rock. He loved it. He absolutely adored it, and he would talk to me about it for hours at a time, while we were supposed to be working. He told me about an establishment in town called Moran's Hotel, in the basement of which there were punk-rock concerts almost every night. Hubert seemed to know a lot about punk rock. It was all about being "against society", he said. It was about "smashing the system". He himself was "against society", he assured me. There were legions of people in the basement of Moran's Hotel every night of the week who were also "against society", and they had stuck safety pins through their ears, cheeks and noses to prove it.

The bands who played in Moran's Hotel were against society too, all of them. But the worst of the lot, Hubert confided, the mankiest shower of louse-ridden, no-good, low-down bowsies ever to plug in a Marshall, ram up the volume and hammer out a three-chord trick, was a band called the Boomtown Rats. They were "fuckin' scum", Hubert would say. He would smile in a fondly contented way when he said this, as though attaining the state of fuckin' scumhood was something in which a person could take considerable pride. "They don't even fuckin' wash themselves," he would beam. How he was in a position to know such a thing was never revealed.

I would have loved to go to Moran's Hotel, of course, but being under-age I couldn't. Yet I was frantically curious about this crowd of festering reprobates, the Boomtown Rats. I wondered what they would be like. The only live act I had ever seen before was Gary Glitter, performing in a television studio at RTÉ. I wondered if these Boomtown Rats could possibly be as entertaining as Gary. One day Hubert told me that I would soon have a chance to find out. The Boomtown Rats had been booked to play a big outdoor show in Dalymount Park soccer ground. There must have been a bit of a run on gee-shots that week, because Hubert had bought me a ticket as a present.

That August afternoon, having lied to my mother about my destination – I think I said I was going to a boy scouts' day out – I went to the concert with Hubert and his girlfriend Mona. Mona was a healthy-looking girl, with the arms of a docker and a bewildering vocabulary of swear words. It was a very hot day and the stadium was packed full of people. Thin Lizzy and Fairport Convention were headlining the concert, but I did not care about that, mainly because Hubert had said these bands were not sufficiently "against society". So, like him and Mona, I only cared about the Boomtown Rats. When their arrival was announced over the PA, I thought Hubert was going to ascend body and soul into heaven, Virgin Mary-wise, so screechingly enthusiastic did he become.

I had never experienced anything quite like the excitement as the band sloped onto the stage, picked up their instruments and began to play. I felt as though a lightning storm was flickering through my nerve endings. It's something you never really forget, the first time you hear the scream of an electric guitar, the thud of a bass or the clash of a real high-hat cymbal. The lead singer, Bob Geldof, looked like a skinny and drooling demon, as he leapt and tottered around the boards, spitting out lyrics into his microphone. The keyboard player, Johnny "Fingers" Moylett, wore pyjamas on stage, an act of the most unspeakable and unprecedented sartorial anarchy. The bassist, Pete Briquette, lurched up and down leering dementedly, as though suffering from a particularly unpleasant strain of BSE. And if guitarists Gerry Cott and Gary Roberts, and drummer Simon Crowe, looked relatively normal, you still would have had not inconsiderable reservations about the prospect of any one of them babysitting your sister.

They played their music frantic and fast, incredibly LOUD, with a curious mixture of passion, commitment and utter disdain for the audience. I loved them. I had never heard a noise like this in my life. I was nailed to the ground by it. When they thrashed into their first single, "Looking After Number One", I swear to you, every single hair on my body stood up and promptly did the Mashed Potato.

Now, this was what I called music. I went home that night with my head pounding and my heart reeling. My mother was waiting, of course, and she spent several hours yelling at me, which made my headache even worse. But I felt empowered by the music, I really did. It sounds so naive now, I know, but that's the way it was. I felt that I had witnessed a kind of revelation. I felt that life was actually very simple. All you had to do, if someone was getting on your case, was tell them to fuck off, that you didn't want to be like *them*, that you wanted to be like YOU! I told my mother this and she didn't exactly see things my way, to put it mildly. But it was the summer of 1977, you see. It all seemed very simple.

Back in school, in September, I told my friends all about the Boomtown Rats. I had five friends: Andrew McK, Andrew D, Nicky, Conor and John. I think we were friends because nobody else liked us. Also, John's parents were separated, like my own, and Conor's mother had died, as had Andrew D's father. So we felt we had something in common, in some odd way. I think we felt we had experienced more interesting pain than other people. Of course, being teenage boys, we didn't talk much about such things. It turned out that Conor, a shy and very good-looking fellow, had heard about the Boomtown Rats himself. He had read an article about them – he was the one of our group who used to read articles. It transpired that several members of the band, Bob Geldof and Johnny Fingers included, had actually *been to our school.*

If I had been interested in the Rats before, my enthusiasm rocketed through the roof now. These anti-establishment scumbags had actually been to *my school.* Blackrock College, the alma mater of Irish President Éamon de Valera. This priest-run joint that had always been famous for taking in the sons of the Dublin middle class and churning out obedient wage-slaves – had somehow produced the Boomtown Rats! How had this possibly happened? There was hope for us all, it seemed.

Now, Irish readers must forgive me for a moment while I explain something to others. There is a television programme in Ireland called *The Late Late Show*. Its former host, Gay Byrne, is a genial man of polite manners and generally mild views. It is often jokingly said in Ireland that Gaybo is the most powerful man in the country. Like many jokes in Ireland – as opposed to Irish jokes – this contains the seed of a profound truth. One evening that autumn, Bob Geldof and the Rats were booked to appear on *The Late Late Show*. Once again, I lied to my mother, so that I could get out of the house and go up to my friend's house to watch it.

The atmosphere in my friend's living room was electric as we uncapped the shandy bottles, passed around the solitary spit-soaked cigarette and waited for the Messiah to descend. Bob shambled onto the screen like an bedraggled wino and sneered his way through the interview in a furtive southside drawl. He detested many things about Ireland, he said. He loathed the Catholic Church; he hated the priests who had taught him in Blackrock College; he disliked his father. He had only gotten into rock and roll in order to get drunk and get laid. Almost everything he said was greeted with horrified gasps and massed tongue-clickings from the audience, and wild cheers from myself and my friends. When the interview was over, the rest of the band came on and performed "Mary of the Fourth Form", a feverish song about the seduction of a schoolteacher by a female student. As the number climaxed in a clamour of drums and wailing feedback, the studio audience was absolutely stunned.

"Well done, Bob," smiled Gay Byrne, ever the professional. Geldof turned around, scowling, wiping the saliva from his lips with the back of his hand. "Yeah, well, if you liked it so much," he snapped, "just go and buy the record." Fuck! The guy was giving cheek to Gay Byrne now! Well, this was something new and dangerous. This was practically revolution.

In Ireland in the late 1970s, this was absolutely astounding talk. This was the decade when one million people – a third of the entire population of the state – had attended a Mass said by the Pope in Dublin's Phoenix Park. This was many years before Mary Robinson, or the introduction of divorce, or legalisation for gay rights in Ireland. You could not legally buy a condom in Ireland in the late 1970s, never mind go on the television and talk so blithely about getting drunk and getting laid and hating priests and disliking your father. And although I liked my own father a great deal,

Geldof's pungent cocktail of motor-mouth arrogance, somewhat unwise trousers and utter disrespect for authority really did appeal to me. In time, I couldn't get enough of it.

Soon after *The Late Late Show*, my friend Conor got a copy of the Boomtown Rats' first record and he taped it for me. It wasn't really punk. It wasn't punk at all, in fact; it was just souped-up rhythm and blues played with a lot of aggression. But there were some fantastic songs on it. "Never Bite the Hand That Feeds" and "Neon Heart", for instance. The music was raw, brimming with verve and a crisp visceral energy. But there were other things I admired about it. The songs were full of characters. I liked that. It made the songs seem like they were about real people. And there was a surprising facility for language, a gutsy pared-down approach to storytelling.

But on the Boomtown Rats' first record there was also a slow piano-based ballad called "I Can Make It If You Can". It was a tender song of vulnerability and longing. I kept the tape beside my bed, and I would put on "I Can Make It If You Can" every morning as soon as I woke up. I felt that this was the voice of a survivor, a guy who knew about pain. I felt he was singing to me, and to people like me, and that there was an integrity to what he was singing about. I played the tape until it wore out and couldn't be played any more. And there were many mornings around that time, I don't mind saying it, when that song really helped me to get out of bed. I can make it if you can.

The thing is, I used to get very down in those days. It began as pretty typical adolescent stuff but it got steadily worse, until it got more serious, until it became real depression. I missed my brother and my two sisters. I missed my father more than I can say, and I wasn't getting on at all well with my mother. I was supposed to go and see my father every weekend, but my mother had gotten to the stage where she would simply not let me do this. She had begun to drink too much. She was also taking drugs – sleeping pills and tranquillisers of various kinds. She must have been enduring some dreadful pain, the poor woman. At the time, I must say, I only cared about the suffering she was inflicting on me. Her temper, when she lost it, became ferocious and unpredictable. Sometimes she would even try to turn me against my father, and against my brother and sisters. She would insist that I was not to go and see my dad. Most of the time I wouldn't go, because I wanted a quiet life. And often when we did meet – he won't mind me saying it – my father and I had to meet in secret. A father and son, having to meet in secret, in an Ireland that never tired of spouting platitudes about family values. It's a shame things had to be like that.

I was so full of fear in those days that I would often feel fear clenched up inside me, like a fist, literally, like a physical thing. My life sometimes felt meaningless. In time, it actually got so I could see very little future at all for myself. It is a terrible thing to feel so hopeless when you're so young, but I did for a while, and I have to tell you that honestly.

If my memory is inaccurate on this point, then I ask for forgiveness in advance. But thinking back now, I truly do not think that any teacher, priest or neighbour ever lifted a finger to help my family. There were three things, and three things only, that kept me going throughout my early years. Chief among these was the nurturing love and support of my father, which was constantly and unselfishly given to me and to my siblings, again and again throughout those years and since. He never abandoned me, despite what he was going through himself. The second was the support of my brother, my sisters, my stepmother and my friends. And the third was Bob Geldof.

I would listen to his song "I Can Make It If You Can", and I would believe it. I simply felt that I could make it if Bob Geldof could. I was naive enough to think that, but I'm grateful now for the naivety of youth. I associated myself with Bob Geldof. He would never *ever* get ground down by anything, I felt. If I remembered that, neither would I. As time went on, I began to think more about Bob Geldof. It was the only thing I could do. I derived an active *personal* pleasure from everything the Boomtown Rats got up to. I bought everything they released – "She's So Modern", "Like Clockwork", then the album, *A Tonic for the Troops*. I really did think their success had something to do with me. I felt I was involved in it, inextricably linked to it, bound up with it in ways that nobody but I could understand. I felt they were singing to me. I thought of them as my friends, even though I had never met them. Isn't that funny?

In November 1978, anyway, the Boomtown Rats became the first-ever Irish group to get to the top of the British charts. On *Top of the Pops* that week, as he jabbered the words of "Rat Trap" into his mike, Geldof shredded up a poster of Olivia Newton-John and John Travolta, whose twee single "Summer Nights" the Rats had just ousted from the number one slot. In school, my friends and myself were speechless with joy. Conor cut a photograph of Geldof out of *Hot Press* and we stuck it up in the Hall of Fame, where the framed images of all the famous past pupils of the school had been hung. We stuck Bob up there, among the bishops and diplomats and politicians who had founded the state in which we lived. His gawky snot-nosed face fitted exactly over a photograph of President de Valera, and this fact had the kind of cheap symbolism that appeals very greatly to fourteen-year-olds. It felt like a victory of sorts at the time, and if I am honest, it still does.

Soon after that, things in the life of my family began to worsen again. My mother took my father to court and somehow won back custody of my two sisters and my brother. It was a decision that would lead to great unhappiness for my family. Some would say it was an amazingly stupid decision by the courts. But in holy Catholic Ireland, bizarre legal opinion too often takes precedent over the rights of terrified children, or it did then, at any rate. Things went from bad to worse in the house. There were constant rows, terrible arguments. My father was routinely denied access to us, and nobody official ever did a thing to help him. And there was fear. We experienced terror, the four of us children. We never knew from one moment to the next how my mother would behave towards us. There were many times when she treated us well, with the affection and love that I know she had for us. But there were other times when she seemed to see us as enemies. At those times, the atmosphere in the house was close to unbearable. I don't know how we got through it. I sure as hell couldn't do it now.

I listened to the Boomtown Rats all the time. I would listen to them for hours on end, and let them send me into a kind of comforting trance. "I Don't Like Mondays", "Diamond Smiles"; I knew the words of their songs off by heart. I would recite them, over and over again in my head, over and over. There were many nights when I went to sleep with the words of "I Don't Like Mondays" rattling around in my head; many mornings when I woke up still silently reciting them, like a prayer.

In December 1979, the Boomtown Rats came back to Ireland. They were supposed to play a big concert in Leixlip, but they had been denied permission by the authorities at the last minute. The Boomtown Rats were seen as dangerous and anti-establishment in Ireland, such was the murderous innocence of the times. The band took the authorities to court, and lost. That Christmas, my parents were back in court, too. I went along with my mother, but the judge told me to leave. When I came out of the court and into the huge circular hall of the Four Courts building in Dublin, I was upset and crying. An odd thing happened, then. Fachtna O'Ceallaigh, the Boomtown Rats' manager, was standing on the other side of the hall with his lawyers. I recognised him from the newspapers. His case was on at the same time as my parents' case. He was just standing there with his hands in his pockets, looking cool as fuck. He might have been wearing sunglasses, although I'm not sure. But I was very glad to see him standing there. I felt it was a good omen. It made me think of Bob.

Christmas was dreadful that year. Terrible. The atmosphere in the house was one of pure fear. Early in the New Year the Rats released – unleashed would be a better word – the single "Banana Republic", which deftly summed up their feelings about Ireland, by now feelings that coincided greatly with my own.

It was a devastating attack on a society whose achievements in posturing cant and hypocrisy had so far outstripped its achievements in morality. It was delivered with force and power, at a time when it needed to be so delivered. Nobody but Geldof would have had the guts to do it. I don't know how anyone else felt about it at the time, and to be absolutely frank, I don't care. I admired Geldof for calling it the way he saw it, and I still do admire him for that.

But it was to be the last big single for the Boomtown Rats. Not long after "Banana Republic", things started to wane. There were rumours of drug-taking in and around the band; I don't know if they were true or not. One way or the other, I think the Rats simply began to lose their way as the tastes of the record-buying public started to change. But I still chart where I was in those days, and what I was doing, by remembering their singles. "Elephant's Graveyard" was January 1981, the month after my parents' last court case. "Go Man Go" was August 1981, just before my eighteenth birthday, the month my mother had to go into hospital for a fortnight.

We never told my father about my mother's absence. Instead, we stayed in the house by ourselves and we went pretty wild. We stayed up late, we did exactly what we liked, we painted the words BOOMTOWN RATS across the front doors of our garage. We were drunk with freedom. We practically trashed the house. We moved four matt-resses into one room, and we slept there, with the door locked. That's the kind of dread we had. We left the Boomtown Rats on loud, almost all the time. That's what I remember now, the blankness in the eyes of my siblings, the intoxicating light-headedness of fear and freedom, the thud of the bass coming up through the floorboards, the nasal roar of Geldof's voice. When you are in trouble, it is odd where you find consolation.

When my mother came home from hospital, it was clear that things could never be the same again in the house. We had tasted something like liberation, and would not easily go back to being suppressed. One Sunday afternoon, three weeks after she came home, my two sisters ran away and returned to live with my father, where they were treated with the love, affection and respect they deserved. They never came back to Glenageary.

"Never in a Million Years" was released in November 1981, just after I started college. That month, things got too much for me at home and I moved out too. My father helped me to get a flat near college. I made some good friends in university, but I wasn't happy. I had the habit of telling people barefaced lies in those days, for pretty much no reason at all. I think it was something to do with our former existence at home. It had been an environment where lies had become the norm for survival, and where the truth was often to be feared. So I hurt some of the new friends I had made by carrying this bizarre approach to the notion of truth out into the real world. I also felt ripped apart with guilt and self-loathing for leaving my brother. I sometimes went to meet him in the afternoons. He attended a school just down the road from the campus but, as had been the case with my father, we had to keep our meetings secret. One day when I went to see him he had brought along the copy of *A Tonic for the Troops* which I had left in my mother's house on the day I had finally run away. That tore me to pieces, I don't know why.

"House on Fire" was released in February 1982, when I was going out with a girl called Grace Porter. "Charmed Lives" was June the same year, just after we broke up. "Nothing Happened Today" was August 1982, just after I finished my first-year exams. Almost everything that happened to me in those days I am able to mark with a song by the Boomtown Rats. They may not be the greatest records ever made, but they're memorable to me because they were involved with my life, and with the things I was doing, and with the people I knew and cared about.

The single "Drag Me Down" came out in May 1984. I remember this because I bought it one cold afternoon in Dún Laoghaire Shopping Centre, before getting the bus up to Glenageary to visit my mother. She was surprised to see me; she seemed pleased at first. We talked for a while, although I don't recall much about what was said.

I remember she asked me if I had a girlfriend now. I said no, I didn't, for some reason, although in truth I did. I smoked a cigarette in front of her, and she was shocked that I was smoking. We had an argument, then, and we parted on bad terms. It was the last time I ever saw her. My mother died nine months later in a car crash.

It was a Sunday morning. She was driving to Mass.

I went to Nicaragua that summer. I was utterly bewildered and confused about my mother's death. I couldn't really figure out what to feel about it, besides a grief of such depth that I couldn't understand it. I think I was probably a bit crazy, and longing to find some kind of frame into which I could fit the events of the last few years more clearly. So I ran away to Nicaragua to be by myself. I took a tape of the Boomtown Rats' last album, *In the Long Grass*, and also a tape of their last ever single, "A Hold of Me". In some ways I wanted to forget about home, and in other ways I wanted to remember every last thing.

But it's odd, the stuff that happens. One of the first people I met in Nicaragua was Lyn Geldof, one of Ireland's leading journalists, and also Bob's sister. She's a terrific woman, very smart and bright and funny, and I was lucky enough to get to know her a little bit while I was there. Now, Bob had said some pretty critical things about his family life, but he hadn't ever spoken about Lynn much. I thought she was really lovely, and that Bob was very lucky to have a sister like that.

That was the summer of Live Aid. Many people with left-wing views were uncomfortable with the idea of the project, and I was one of them, I have to admit. I felt that charity wasn't the best way to deal with the problems of the developing world. Maybe I was right, maybe I was wrong, I don't know any more. Like Woody Allen said, don't ask me why there were Nazis, I can't even get the can-opener to work. What I do know is that Geldof was clearly motivated by nothing but humanity. If those critics on the Left who took cheap shots at him had displayed something like the same humanity, both in their criticisms and in their politics, the world would be a better place.

I came back to Ireland and returned to college. Slowly, gradually, things began to calm down a bit in my life. But I often thought about the old days, and sometimes when I did, the Boomtown Rats would come into my mind. Their career seemed to have petered out by that stage. Geldof was probably the most famous person in the world, but the band hadn't made a record in a long time, and they seemed to have no plans to do so.

In May 1986, amid rumours that the band was about to call it a day for good, they came back to Dublin to play at a charity event, featuring Van Morrison, U2, The Pogues – all the great and the good of the Irish rock world. The Rats played a stormer. They blew everyone away and received a tumultuous reception from the audience. After the main set, Geldof strolled up to the microphone for an encore. He seemed taken aback by the warmth of the crowd's affection. At first – unusually – he didn't seem to know what to say. He appeared a little lost as his eyes ranged over the crowd.

"Well, it's been a great ten years," he muttered. "So, rest in peace."

The thundering drum roll began. The opening riff pounded out. The familiar chords: D, A, G, E. The last song the Boomtown Rats ever played in public was their first song, Geldof's hymn to snot-nosed anarchy and adolescent attitude, "Looking After Number One".

It was at once a powerful homecoming, a stylishly ironic act of self-deprecation and a poignant farewell. And in some odd and quite profound sense, it seemed like a farewell to me, too, a final goodbye to a time in my life that was over now. As I watched the show on television that day, I knew that I would leave Ireland again soon, that I would not come back for a long time, and that I would try to forget about most of my past.

I came to England four months after that. I went to Oxford to do a doctorate, didn't like it much, and dropped out. I came to London then, decided to stay there because I liked its anonymity, its vast size. All the things that other people hated about London, I loved. It was a great place in which to get lost, and that's what I did for a while – just kept to myself and got lost.

Gradually I lost touch with my old schoolfriends. I had ups and downs in my personal life, times of great joy, too. I moved flat three or four times, and somewhere along the way I left behind all my old Boomtown Rats records. But I remember their force and power still, the healing power of their righteous indignation. And I suppose that sometimes the words don't seem quite as electrifying now as they did in Dalymount Park on a summer day when I was thirteen years old and breathless with discovery. But that doesn't bother me much. Because great pop music sometimes heals us in ways that we don't understand, or in ways that seem unbelievably trite or trivial when we look back. Great pop music is about the people who listen to it, and the circumstances in which they do so, and not really in the end about the people who make it. Maybe that's what's so great about it, I don't know.

A few years ago I wrote a novel called *Cowboys and Indians*, about the love of rock music, among other things. In the winter of 1991, after a reading I did in Dublin, a girl I used to know in the old days came up to me and said that my friend Conor, who had given me my first Boomtown Rats tape, was dead. Things hadn't worked out for him in Dublin, she said. He had left Ireland, like so many of the young people I knew. He had drifted around for a while, ended up in Paris, and had been happy enough there. But then something bad had happened to him – she didn't know what exactly – and he had died.

I was so shocked. I could not believe what had happened. I had a lot to drink and I lay awake for hours, just thinking about the past, unrolling images from my child-hood as though looking at a film. I cried that night. When finally I fell asleep I dreamed about poor Conor. Sometimes – very occasionally – I dream about him still. When I do, it's always the same happy dream. I see his laughing shy face on the day we stuck the photograph of Bob Geldof up in the Hall of Fame in Blackrock College. I hear him whispering, "Let's do it, Joe. Come on, don't be afraid." It's not the worst way to remember him. And I'm sure the Boomtown Rats are up on the wall in Blackrock College officially now. But we beat the authorities to it, me and my friend Conor. We beat them by a whole decade.

Two years ago, I was on a television programme in Ireland to talk about my novel, and Bob Geldof was one of the guests. I was extremely apprehensive about meeting him, because he had been such a hero of mine. He was connected to so many painful memories, I suppose, and I've met enough pop stars to know that they usually have the intelligence quotient of a piece of toast. But he was absolutely great. He had the air of a survivor. He seemed like a man who had come through.

In the green room after the show, he introduced me to his sister Cleo, and to his father. (He described his father as "the real Bob Geldof".) He was very polite to everybody, and he made real efforts to include people in the conversation. We chatted for a while about nothing at all, his eyes flitting around the room as he talked, his hands running through his straggly hair. When the time came to go I asked him if he wanted to come out for a jar, but he said no. He was going out for a meal with his family. So we shook hands and he got his stuff together and sloped from the room with his father and his sister, a guitar case under his arm. It was like watching a part of your past walk out the door.

I never got the chance to tell him what was on my mind that night. There were too many people around. Anyway, I suppose I hadn't really found the words I was looking for. But when I think about it now, what I wanted to say was actually very simple. It was this: I didn't have the worst childhood in Ireland by any means. I had some things that other kids could only have dreamed about. I had them because people who loved me worked hard and made sacrifices to ensure that I would. For those blessings I am grateful and always will be. But there were bad things, too. There were dark days. I don't say it to blame or to hate, just to acknowledge that there were very dark days. Just to tell that truth. We in Ireland need to tell the truths of our past if we are to build up the decent and compassionate home that all our children deserve to live in. This country could be an absolutely wonderful place. For me, it wasn't always. And Bob Geldof helped me through. When I was a scared kid, who felt that there was little point to life, his music and his example were second only to the love of my father and my stepmother and my brother and sisters in keeping me going through all the terror and misery. It helped me survive. It helped me sit out the dark days, and wait for the better times to come. They did come. They often do. And I don't care whether nobody likes the music now. Tastes change, and times change, and so they should. Besides, a hell of a lot of people didn't like it then. But *I* did. Big time. His music embodied a world-view to which I felt some connection. It opened my eyes to things that had never occurred to me before. Like the greatest pop music, it was fun, unpredictable, alive, iconoclastic, intelligent, witty, danceable, tender when it wanted to be, tough as nails when it had to be. It just made me feel better. It healed. And it made me think I could make it, if *he* could. A foolish and adolescent belief, if ever there was one. But in a world where I had to grow up too fast, at least Bob Geldof and his band allowed me to be foolish and adolescent just once in a while.

I'm grateful indeed, for that little, or that much. I'm very grateful for that.

The Secret World of the Irish Mammy

A few years ago St Patrick's Day and Mother's Day happened to fall on the same Sunday. Well a thing like that can make you think. Particularly if you can't be bothered to get out of bed.

What do we really feel about mothers here in Mother Ireland, the world capital of po-faced devotion to mammydom? Oh yes, we sing about the mammy when we're rat-faced drunk and we bung her a bunch of daffodils every Mother's Day morning, which we stole from the forecourt of a garage down the road. And musha, why wouldn't we? She's our mammy, after all.

Many traditional Irish ballads celebrate the special role of mothers, including the following beautiful and poignant example from the 1920s in South Kerry. It is sung to the tune of "Spancil Hill", with a tremendously deep feeling of beer:

> *Oh Mammy, you're a livin' saint,*
> *An angel in a dress.*
> *You always have a lovely smile*
> *When you're sweepin' up the mess.*
> *When I'm loadin' up me weapon, boys,*
> *For to aim it at a Brit,*
> *I think about me mammy's smile.*
> *And I shoot the little shit.*[1]

Such stirring examples of native song expressed our patriotic feelings about the Mammyland. And our mammies had a

---

[1] Quoted in *Five Hundred Songs of Mother Ireland* by Dr Oedipus O'Beard (Maam Cross Publications).

unique place in our affections. For example, as Gemma Hussey's book *Ireland: Anatomy Of A Changing State* points out, if you look up the word "mother" in the index to the 1937 Constitution, the document on which every single Irish law is predicated, you will notice the words, "*Woman – see family and sex*".

Nice, huh?

Must have been really convenient for Irish mammies to be shown with such clarity just what they were for.

Oh begob, we were historically, hysterically, mad about the mammy. On Mother's Day we cooked the lunch. Well OK, *she* actually cooked it the day before but at least we managed to heat it up without setting fire to the kitchen. Because we *loved* our mammy. We LOVED HER TO DEATH. And just to really prove our love, a Dáil motion of 1925 stopped her getting divorced; a law of 1927 excluded her from jury service. Well, we didn't want our mammies sitting in the courts or anything. Sure it's *men* who decide what crimes are, not ladies! And when it came to setting up the Censorship Board, our mammies were once again excluded. We wouldn't want our mammies reading dirty literature, vile sweaty guff about lezzers and malcontents. It might take their minds off washing our pants.

Strangely enough, a great number of books which the male censors thought were acceptable promoted an image of our mammies as victims or virgins. But that didn't worry us. "Sit back there, Mammy, it's Mother's Day," we cried. "Here's a box of chocolates and a few balls of wool. Would you ever knit me another jumper?" Our mammies were helpfully banned from the civil service in 1925, to allow them more time to clean up our bedrooms. Ten years later they were told they couldn't have any of those nasty English contraceptives. We liked them being our mammies so much, we decided they should be mammies over and over again!

Yes, we sent her a card every year. It expressed our gratitude and profound appreciation in heart-warmingly sentimental little verses such as the following:

Mammy, how I thank you;
You really are my friend;
All the love you give me –
Love without end.
And when you get to Paradise,
Our Lord Himself will say:
"Welcome, dearest Mammy –
NOW WHERE'S ME SHAGGIN'
TAY?!"[2]

OK, so we didn't *always* feel as well-disposed as that. Occasionally we thought our mammies were getting strange modern ideas. We didn't like some of the clothes they wore. When a mammy is a mammy she

[2] William Butler Yeats, *The Song of the Wandering Mammy.*

should *dress* like a mammy. So we got the Bishops to write a few pastoral letters about "immodest fashions in female dress". And the priests would put on their nice lacey frocks and flowing silken gowns and read to our mammies from the altar, telling them not to be dressing like tarts.

By 1937 the Bishops were busy with other things. Yes, they were happily writing the new Constitution with the occasional bit of interference from the actual government. There were three TDs at the time who were mammies. But these were naughty, *unhelpful* mammies. They wouldn't just shut up and make the sandwiches, the way a proper mammy should. No, they kept on making speeches, yapping out of them – you know the way the ladies do. They went so far as to claim that mammies had rights! Well we had to talk a bit of sense into them. So we got the newspapers to do that for us.

Here is an absolutely genuine quote from an *Irish Independent* editorial of the time:

Many men (including, it is whispered, the President) think that a woman cuts a more fitting and more useful figure when darning the rents in her husband's socks by the fireside than she could hope to cut in a Parliamentary assembly…

Now. That softened their cough for them, didn't it? We didn't send *those* mammies a Mother's Day card. Naughty mammies. *Bad* mammies.

For thirty years after that, there was barely a peep out of the happy Irish mammy. She was busy at home, where she needed to be. She had fourteen children, after all. And every Mother's Day we brought her breakfast in bed, where she was happily giving birth to the next babby while simultaneously ironing us a shirt in which to emigrate. All this feminist nonsense about our mammies being oppressed. All that liberal hokum about miscarriage and stillbirth rates being the highest in Europe. Our mammies *loved* their wonderful lives. And didn't they have their own mammy in heaven – The *Blessed* Mammy – to put in a word for them when things got a bit tiring?

No, the Irish mammy had a wonderful time. On Mother's Day, Daddy would give her a little break. Or sometimes even a compound fracture. But that was a terribly rare occurrence. In fact no Irish mammy *ever* had to live in a violent marriage, so there was no need at all to give them legal aid, or change the laws to allow them to have abusive husbands removed. So that was handy! They were *never* deserted or abandoned with their children, so the taxpayer never had to give them welfare. Think of all the money we saved! As for the few *very* bad mammies who did run out on their husbands just for punching them every night for ten years – well you will always get the rotten apple. (As Eve found out.) But even *then* we didn't turn our backs on them. Oh no. In order to protect that misguided mammy, the Criminal Conversation laws were introduced, entitling her ape-like geek of a husband to prosecute anyone who gave her a cup of tea and a sandwich. I ask you, what could be fairer than that? *Every* day was Mother's Day here in Ireland!

Admittedly our mammies were considered their husbands' property. But that was what our mammies *wanted*. And what man in his right senses wouldn't look after such a valuable possession? This is what the young women of today completely fail to understand – our mammies didn't *mind* that until 1965 they could be disinherited by their husbands. Not at all. They thought it was great! And they didn't *mind* that they weren't entitled to the dole, or that their only legal status was as dependents of males, or that Children's Allowance payments were made to fathers and not mothers. And as for getting equal pay for equal work?

They were mammies, for God's sake! *Their* work was being walked on!

Late last year, I was listening to Marian Finucane's radio programme, when a young woman called to say she wanted to take up boxing but was having difficulty finding a trainer. Would any of the listeners have any advice? A much older soft-spoken woman rang to say she found the idea utterly horrifying. It was undignified, common; so unladylike.

"I mean, Marian," she implored. "Can you imagine the Blessed Virgin Mary in a boxing ring?"

I have to confess I found the picture intriguing. *"In the Red Corner, ladies and gentlemen, wearing the black trunks, the undefeated heavyweight champion of the world – Iron Mike TYSON! (Booooo.) And in the Blue Corner and wearing the sky-blue veil, tonight's contender – something of a newcomer but she's full of grace, an immaculate little mover with some good combinations. Make no assumptions, she's virgin on a title! Your appreciation please – FOR THE MOTHER OF GOD!"*

Now that would be a fight worth getting Sky for.

Ms Finucane had to point out that young Irish women did *lots* of things these days which it might be hard to imagine the Blessed Virgin Mary doing. As indeed they do. Things like vote. Or watch *Ally McBeal* on a Wednesday night. Or employ other modes of transport than assback. It was a funny moment. But it was poignant too.

The historian Dr Margaret McCurtain has remarked, "Around Irishwomen, as in a cage, were set the structures of family life."

You won't be seeing that on a Mother's Day card.

Nor the words of the great Irish socialist, Hannah Sheehy-Skeffington: "Ireland will never be free until Irish women are free."

But sure there you go. That's women for you now. Never bleeding happy, are they?

Letter to Myself at Age Four

Dear Four-Year-Old Self,

Hi. This is me. That's to say, this is *you* plus forty-one years. I'm writing to you from September 2008. Hope you're doing OK back there in 1967? How are the 1960s treating you generally? Are there flowers in your hair? Have you been rioting about Vietnam and the lack of civil rights, or is that disgruntled noise you're making only the result of belated teething? The Beatles released a pretty good record this year, didn't they? It's called *Sergeant Pepper*. Some say it has a future.

So we've a lot to catch up on. What's all my news? Well, I'm married. Seriously. *Yes*, to a girl. I know you're not too crazy about them, but that might change. My wife sometimes tells me I have the mentality of *you*, especially when I'm eating with my mouth open or telling her a joke or leaving my clothes all over the bedroom floor. So it's nice that we're similar. You and me, I mean. Little bit chubby, aren't you? Hey that's great, *so am I*! You're prone to the odd tantrum when you don't get your own way? Well, I got news for you, kiddo… But never mind.

So I have a son of your age, and another who's eight, and both of them seem so much more confident and happy than you do. You're frightened by the whole world, as how would you not be? That's what the world is for, you believe. Most people in the Ireland around you believe pretty much the same thing. It's one nation under the thumb.

What can I tell you about 2008? Well, we have this thing called the *internet*. It's a system someone invented a few years ago, of joining up every computer in the world for the greater good of the planet and the species, and bringing all of humanity together. Well, mainly it's used for acquiring pornography and gambling. So really we've made a lot of progress.

You don't even have colour television, I know. If you did, your parents would actually have to get their backsides up off the sofa in order to change the channels, or the *stations*, as they are called in your 1967 world. No, *Wanderley Wagon* isn't on RTÉ television any more. We have sort of more advanced ideas of what constitutes entertainment now. There's this show called *Fáilte Towers*, right? You'd love it. It's absolutely made for you. It's where people pretend to run a hotel and viewers give them money for charitable causes. Like hospitals for children and help for patients with Alzheimer's and people with autism or cancer or MS. No, no, the government doesn't do that. Don't be such a baby. For God's sake, what are you, four?

Oh yeah, I forgot. Ireland is a prosperous and self-confident country now. Don't laugh in your Liga. It's true! I swear. We drive SUVs and jeeps. Those are cars meant for farmers or soldiers going into battle. No, we're not all farmers. In fact very few of us are farmers, anymore. And we're not going into battle. I don't know why we need military vehicles to drive to the shops. Don't be asking such childish questions.

Anyway – the reason I'm writing is that this week my son who's your age is starting in school. And for some reason, it got me thinking of you. Isn't that funny? Big day for you, wasn't it? You probably found it a scary experience. Yes, your teacher, Mother Lawrence, seems a bit tough, I know. No she isn't your mother, she's just called Mother by the other nuns. And she probably wasn't always called Lawrence. At least, I don't think so. Yes, those ladies dressed in black robes are nuns – that's right. There are thousands of them in your Ireland, you see them every day. Nuns on the beach. Nuns in Clery's. Nuns in the audience of *The Late Late Show* waving shyly or gleefully at the camera. Great flocks of Carmelites, Sisters of Mercy, flying around your childhood like birds. No, we don't have as many of those here in 2008. And the ones we do have wear cardigans. The people dressed in black robes these days are called tribunal barristers. The Sisters of Mercy are a punk-rock group.

But you should listen to Mother Lawrence. She knows what's what. Okay, I know she's a bit fierce. But she'll be teaching you to read. And that's going to bring a lot of happiness and pleasure to your life. You mightn't think it now, but you're going to be endlessly grateful to that woman, for her patience, and yes – her love. Okay, so she doesn't do self-esteem. What's self-esteem, you ask me? Oh, self-esteem means generally not despising yourself or believing you're the Antichrist. It isn't thought too useful in the Ireland you're growing up in. Mother Lawrence hasn't heard of it. Nobody has, really. It would be illegal if anyone had.

So I'd better sign off. You'll be busy, I know. The first week of school can be frightening and confusing. This is just to say, it gets better. My son — your son — is a beautiful boy. He looks like you in photographs. Just less frightened; more smiling. There are times I put my arms around him and feel ghosts are in the room. Take care of yourself, kiddo. You're not alone.

A Francis Street Boy

There's been a lot of talk recently about hard times, new challenges. I find it's got me thinking about my father. Sean was born in 1938, in the Liberties of Dublin, the city's oldest neighbourhood. It was a place of great independence and amazing histories, near the stern black cathedral where Swift had thundered the gospel, near Thomas Street Church, where Robert Emmet was executed. In Sean's childhood and teens there was mass emigration, a sense of the celestial irrelevance of the poor to the fantasies of the Republic they lived in. It was a different world, a different time. The Celtic Tiger would have been unimaginable.

An oaten aroma drifted up from the brewery and the barges plied the Liffey, bringing barrels of Guinness to the world beyond a child's imagination. A city boy, he loved animals, especially birds; he roamed about the Liberties exploring. The grid through which he moved had its landmarks and lighthouses – Saint Nicholas of Myra church, Francis Street School, Meath Street, the Coombe, Johnny Rae's ice-cream shop – place-names that will mean much to all who hailed from the Liberties. The map of an Irish childhood.

Francis Street, now, has antique shops and cappuccino-bars. But in the years of Sean's childhood it wasn't like that. He grew up in a safe home where there were strong values of loyalty and family, where music was valued, and reading, and dependability; keeping your word; being there for one another. But in the streets beyond that home he saw barefoot children, parents beyond coping, hard sights. A restless, questioning boy, he had a talent for English at school. It was an ability encouraged by his beautiful sisters, who adored him. My aunts bought paperback novels and shared them among themselves. Indeed, such hungry readers were those gorgeous young Dubliners that when one of them would become impatient for her turn with the paperback, another would sometimes tear out a page and pass it across the kitchen table. Often you had five or six siblings all reading the same book, each on a different chapter. A magazine, *The Bell*, containing short stories and poetry, was often in the house, and Sean availed of it. He was the sort of boy who enters contests, learns definitions, runs in races, gets sometimes into fights, feels promises deeply, believes the answer to almost anything can be found in a book and is sometimes impatient as a wasp. I see him in many Irish men and women of his own generation.

And I see him in my own beautiful sons, in my brothers and sisters. And I am happy when I see him in myself.

He left school at the age of thirteen and worked to help support his family. Later, as a young father, he dived into his books again. He studied at night, did exams, worked by day, in time qualifying as a structural engineer. He opened a little practice in Dublin and in time it grew. He had a kind of mantra of determination you'd often hear him saying: "Feck them all bar Nelson." (Only he didn't say "feck".) I remember once, as a teenager, asking him, "Dad, why not feck Nelson too?" He replied: "Because, son, he's fecked already."

Churches, schools, office blocks, libraries – they formed themselves on the drawing board he kept at the house. Often, when I went to bed, he would be working at that board, in shirtsleeves, his tie flung over his shoulder. And often in the mornings, as I got ready for school, he would be there again – his eyes raw with tiredness. It seemed to me, as it may have seemed to him, as though he had stood there working all night. He sang as he shaved; little Dublin songs or bits of Italian arias. And at night he would read to me before I slept. He loved the Victorian writers, the old poets like Lord Tennyson. He had been introduced to these poets by Brother Thomas Devane in Francis Street School in the Liberties. I can never read any poem without hearing Sean's beautiful Dublin voice. Calming as a hearth on a rainy night, it was a voice that revealed whole worlds. It was how I had learned to read, or certainly why I wanted to; his finger tracing capitals on the yellowed old pages of books that seemed to breathe wonder into life. That I wanted to be a writer one day, I owe to Sean – to his voice, his love of learning, and of course to his stories.

What fantastic stories he had, but there's one in particular I remember still. It was about a Francis Street boy who bought a goldfish. One day, to see what would happen, he took it out of its bowl, just for the briefest second. And it didn't die! So the next day he took it out for *two seconds*. Still it didn't die. Every day he would take it out, for a little longer each time, until soon he could take the goldfish out of the water for *thirty seconds* and it wouldn't die. He continued like that – one second longer every day. The goldfish got slowly accustomed to these longer periods out of the water. Soon he could take that goldfish out of the water for nearly a full minute, and still it was healthy and well. He was taking the goldfish in its bowl to school one morning, because he wanted to show the teacher this remarkable thing – *a goldfish that can remain out of water for, like, five minutes*! But he stumbled while walking alongside the banks of the canal. And didn't the goldfish fall out of its bowl and into the water. Where it drowned. "And that's a true story," Sean would smile. And somehow, I still believe it is.

And I also believe, without his solidarity and courage, that his life, and therefore mine, would have been different indeed. All my life I have been given chances he did not have. The same is true of many of us. It's hard not to panic when times change very suddenly, as they have for most of us in what seems only a few months. But to read with a child can never be taxed; nor can the belief that there are deeper solidarities than the merely financial. Things were not better in the old days. Nobody sane could say that. But the example of that generation of Irish people has much to offer. It could be a time to remember where we came from.

The Immaculate Conception and Me

One of my earliest December memories is the kindergarten Christmas play when I was four. The story was set on Christmas Eve. Santy was ready to hit the skies with Rudolph, but the weatherman had gone on strike so there was no snow. (No Met Éireann meteorologist this weatherman, but a moody wizard who manufactured the weather from his headquarters at the South Pole.) I played him with the gusto of a high-babies Daniel Day-Lewis. Yeah, I drank that Santy's *milkshake*!

A girl called Niamh was my wife, the weatherwoman. But it wasn't a marriage made in heaven. The plot required that she often hold my hand. Fine; but Niamh had the runniest nose in all Dún Laoghaire, which she persisted in wiping with the same hand that she employed to clutch my own. I draw a veil over the specifics. But let's just say, Niamh and I were bonded by more than love.

Reverend Mother gave me a beard made of cotton wool, and a crêpe-paper smock with spangles glued onto it. The effect was Alvin Stardust meets Osama Bin Laden. Why a nun in 1970s Ireland would have had a false beard, I don't know, and I'm not entirely sure that I want to. The spangles were improvised from the foil tops of milk bottles. The reindeers wore beige tea-towels and were profoundly convincing. Some had cardboard hats with antlers crayoned onto them. The more committed would vigorously attempt reindeer noises. Since few in the greater Dún Laoghaire area had heard a reindeer, creative improvisation was practised. I remember a classmate informing me, with the certainty possessed by toddlers, that a reindeer sounded "exactly like a bat". Alas, I hadn't heard a bat either.

One morning at rehearsal, a confrontation erupted between the shepherds and the Holy Family. A shepherd had called the Virgin Mary a rude name. She had responded with an upper-cut to the chin. Hell broke loose. Never had I witnessed such a mêlée. There were fists, boots, bits of manger being brandished. I recall seeing Saint Joseph bawl at the Bethlehem innkeeper "You're CLAIMED!". The history of Christianity might well have turned out somewhat differently had the real Saint Joseph tried this approach. In the scuffle, one of the Wise Men got sent home for spitting at an Archangel and snapping a leg off Baby Jesus. Baby Jesus was played by Roddy, my lovely eldest sister Eimear's most prized dolly. He had eyes that looked at you crossways, and was devoid of genitalia, so there was enough on his mind already without assaulting him. But I remember the Baby Jesus being hurled across the class-room, before being used to bludgeon one of Santy's elves while she was sat upon by Our Blessed Lady. It's an image that kinda stays with you, somehow. Since then, I've re-garded Christmas as a contact sport. Forget decking the halls. Deck a shepherd instead.

December, in my childhood, was a difficult month anyway, for a reason I remember almost every time I enter a church these days, which doesn't happen as often as it used to back then. For it was on the 8th of December, in 1966, that the younger of my two sisters was born. It's a date that used to see the beginnings of Christmas in Ireland, in the days before we decided it had to start in late August. Country people would come to Dublin to do their shopping for the season. The lights, such as they were, would be switched on. That date is also the feast of the Immaculate Conception, a day of obligation for Catholics. My mother was in hospital, having given birth that very morning. It was my beloved and devout grandmother and my wonderful father who took upon themselves the duty of taking my three-year-old self to Mass. The church was packed – it was a different time in Ireland. We arrived late and stood in the back with many others. When the time came for Communion, my father and grandmother took it in turns to hold me while each of them approached the crowded altar to receive it. I began to feel left out. And I didn't like that feeling. Anyone who was in Glasthule Church, on that December day in 1966, may still remember what happened. During the fervently reverent silence that descended immediately following, the priest approached the tabernacle and piously opened it, replacing the chalice and bowing his head. My three-year-old mouth opened and out came the blood-curdling shriek, "He's lockin' it all away! And I didn't get any!"

It was the beginning of a difficult relationship with Catholicism generally, and I often think it goes back to that moment. As for the beautiful baby who had been born to our family that morning, perhaps few would have expected that one day she would record a song called "Nothing Compares 2 U", which would enter people's memories with such beauty and power. Certainly there is possibility in the air, a little magic in December. And no amount of tinsel and gaudiness and noise can ever truly crush it out.

A Birthday Letter to my Stepmother

Dear Viola,

It can't be easy being anyone's step-mother. From our earliest childhood, the stepmother peoples our fairytales – a woman portrayed almost invariably as wicked, brimming with resentments and cruelties.

There are days when I find it hard to be a good father to my own children. To be a parent to anyone else's seems unimaginable. But that was what you were, and it wasn't always easy. Another woman's frightened children tumbled in and out of your life. We were accepted, helped, minded, reassured. I'm not saying you were a saint. You were something more decent than that. A woman trying to do her best for people who needed her. A woman who would never break a promise.

In caring for a household which, at times, contained eight children, you witnessed plenty of ups and downs. You saw love stories conducted over a telephone at which a queue used to form. The bill must have been the equivalent of a small country's national debt. How many broken hearts did you soothe? How many tales of woe did you endure? You were not given to easy mottos or cheap advice, but I remember you once telling me something that remains with me still: always act with courage when love is at stake. When you're disappointed, be brave. And if you have to disappoint, be braver. Love is not sentiment, the easily repeated nothing; it is commitment and selflessness and patience. It is the acknowledgement, as Iris Murdoch so beautifully wrote, that another human being is real. We don't always remember this fact when we're thinking about the children in our lives. But you and my father did.

Ireland is a country besotted with its myths. In the frightened and obedient society in which I grew up, there was still the widespread idea that a family had one definition: two people who have never been married to anyone else, happily married now, with children they always wanted, probably with a dog and never a disagreement. The picture of contentment personified. Nobody is ever hurt. No feelings have been crushed. No hopes have been trampled. Everything worked out. No one has baggage. Children are always angelic. The good have been rewarded with happiness. The fact that there were so very many of us who did not belong to such a family was forgotten. Those of us who were children of separated couples felt we were the only people in the world to whom this had ever happened. That's the way it was. I don't think I exaggerate. Couples who had separated must have often felt the same way. But, to me, you embodied a truth which has become part of my thinking: that below all the propaganda and lies, there are quieter and very powerful solidarities that arise between people for the most important reason of all – because they should. We're a country full of carers of various kinds; minding the sick, the fragile, the vulnerable, those who need us. There are families we are born into and there are often families we choose, which don't fit the categories, the dictionary definitions. There is no destiny waiting for us, no preordained path. It is rather that those we meet and care for become that destiny. It is only a matter of recognising them.

I don't know that you'd put it like that, or if you ever thought about it much. Probably you were too busy loving us to analyse. But I see now that you made a decision that you would always do your best to stand by us, never leave when things got tough. And when they did get tough, as from time to time they did, I still never saw you break a promise or heard you tell me a lie. Blood may be thicker than water, but we make our own wine. It's the greatest lesson of being a stepson.

This week sees an important birthday for you and I send you my loving thanks, for your wisdom, your gentleness and solidarity. Like my father, you are uncomfortable with being praised, and would always very much rather no fuss was made at all. You like quietness, no atmospheres; things running along in peace. I've known you half your life. You've known me three quarters of mine. Like any other human being, I contain my mother and my father, and theirs, and theirs, all the way into the past, and I am fortunate in having come to see the beauty of everyone who made me. But I don't think I could have done that, had it not been for knowing you. So I consider myself blessed and honoured that you were one of the people who made me. Sometimes it's better to have had two mothers.

A Broken Hallelujah

I suspect that like many parents my most memorable Christmas was the one following the birth of our first child. We had been living in London for some years and that's where the lad was born. But when he was a few months old we returned to live in Dublin, arriving at the start of Christmas week, 2000. The plan had been for my wife and the baby to fly, and I would take our rusting decrepit car on the ferry. But in all the excitement and exhausted happiness and clutter of new parenthood, we left it too late to book a flight and there wasn't a seat to be had.

Thus I remember driving across England in that cold, late December, the last of the twentieth century, the last of a millennium. We drove through fog and sleet and ice-glazed scenery, the wipers relentlessly fighting the hail, and the crackle of the banjaxed radio. The car was older than our relationship, indeed practically on the scrap heap. At some point someone had spilled a pint of milk on the floor. This made the interior smell like Satan's breath. But you couldn't open the window. Being face-whipped by a hailstorm as you're driving past Stoke isn't anyone's idea of air-conditioning. I had actually tried to sell the jalopy in London as a prelude to re-immigration, telling the dealer it had been valued at two and a half grand. He took it out for a brief test drive before handing me back the keys. "Fackin' key-ring's worth more than the car," he said.

My wife was in the back, with a toaster on her lap, a portable telly beneath her feet, and her pockets full of spoons and forks. In my memory, she was wearing almost every exterior garment she possessed (a) because it was so cold, and (b) because we couldn't afford another suitcase. I had entrusted her with the really important things in my life, i.e. my Patti Smith and Clash records. In my memory these were balanced on top of her head, in the manner of a Bedouin woman carrying a water jar from an oasis. In fact she was holding them in her frostbitten fingers, whose tips were turning a fetching shade of blue. Under many layers of clothing I had on my favourite T-shirt, an item purchased in revolutionary Nicaragua in 1985. The T-shirt had lasted longer than the revolution. Oh yeah – the baby was there too, strapped into a safety seat, but a safety seat whose workings neither of us had full confidence we understood because sadly we don't have a degree in Advanced Mechanical Engineering. While into the crock's boot had been packed the remainder of our worldly goods, total value about nine quid fifty.

I was full of mixed feelings about coming back to live in Ireland. Some of the happiest years of my life had been spent in London. I had met my wife there, had many friends and colleagues there, and had always felt strangely at home there, as I think many Irish people do. So why were we going to Dublin? I wasn't quite sure. As our car sputtered across England, my wife started telling me that it was all my idea. I, countering brilliantly, said it had been all *her* idea. At some point we had an argument and I didn't speak to her for an hour. Well, I didn't like to interrupt her. As anyone who has ever undertaken that drive knows well, it's plain sailing through the English midlands, where things like motorways and electric lighting have been heard of. When you cross the border into Wales, the roads start to narrow and snake, and what looks on a map as though it might take you ten minutes can end up taking you forty years. But rural Wales is of course a scenically attractive place, if you don't mind hearing "Duelling Banjos" strike up in your head now and again. I was coughing and spluttering as a result of a bad cold, but it did make my attempts to pronounce those Welsh place-names beginning with two Ls as enjoyable as they were memorably phlegmy. We made it to Holyhead just as they closed the barriers. We were literally the last car allowed to board the ship. If we hadn't had a baby with us I'm not sure the security guards would have taken pity. I had to do an awful lot of bleating and looking vulnerable. As this was before Bertie Ahern's famous interview with Brian Dobson, it was hard to think of someone whose Oliver Twist-demeanour and facial expressions it might be useful to imitate.

It was the midnight sailing, and we rocked across the Irish Sea. It was a dreadful night, the worst crossing I've ever known.

Through all of it, the little one slept soundly in a carry cot on the floor of the lounge. Around us ranted the mobs of beer-fuelled émigrés. They were roaring, carousing, slapping one another on the back, singing carols with obscene lyrics, and trying to garrotte one another with lengths of tinsel. It was like being at a re-enactment of a nineteenth-century *Punch* caricature of Irish people enjoying themselves at a funeral. There were rebel yells and mawkish choruses, screechings, cursings, birdie-songs and boogieing and brandying. That shining pearl of Shane McGowan's genius, "Fairytale of New York" was sung so oft and so badly that I came to hate it with a passion. I don't exaggerate when I tell you that to this very day, I immediately switch off the radio when it comes on. Every time a massive wave hit the ship, we seemed to rise a hundred feet in the air before crashing back down again with the implacable viciousness of a hanging judge's gavel. The gnash of glasses breaking.

The moans of en-masse vomming. I couldn't believe the baby was so tolerant of the punk-rock ambience. If I had never loved him before, which I had, very much, I think I bonded with him that night in some fundamental way. Here was a kid who could sleep through "The Fields of Athenry". Our Dozol bill would always be low.

By six in the morning the party had ended, mainly because most of the celebrants were by now unconscious. Closer to dawn, the baby was still sleeping, comatose as a student. His mum asked me to get her a bottle of water. After I'd done that, I remember asking her if she wanted to go out and get some air on the deck. She didn't really want to, but she suggested I step out myself if I liked.

Everything was calm. It was a cold, clear morning. I don't think I had ever seen a sky that had so many stars, and certainly I never have since. You felt you could touch them, stir them around. There was an unearthliness about the beauty and the stillness. I walked the decks for a while. People were gathered here and there. And as I rounded the stern of the ship, there was an elderly couple who were sharing a flask of tea and listening to classical music on a radio. I don't know if I can convey to you the strange beauty of that scene: being that far out at sea, in the dark and the cold, with haunting music being played on a radio. I stood near them for a while. I think I was smoking. And what happened next, I'll never forget.

A piece of music they recognised came on. And I recognised it too. They turned it up a little and poured themselves another cup of tea. It was an extract from Handel's *Messiah*. You probably know it – you'll have heard it now and again. But you've likely never heard it in the circumstances I describe. The choir began to sing. And the old couple hummed along. And I found I could hardly move.

For unto us,

A child is born.
Unto us,
A son is given.

Now, I should tell you that I am not the kind of feller who easily cries. But when I heard those simple, beautiful words, it was hard to remember that. I stood in the dark and tried hard not to weep. Dawn began to come on. The sky turned red and gold. The ship was by now approaching Dún Laoghaire, the town where I grew up. I could actually see the pier where my pals and I used to hang out on summer evenings, the stretch of coastline at Sandycove, near where I kissed and was kissed for the first time, the steeples and the shopping centre, and Killiney Hill in the distance, its obelisk silhouetted against an impossibly scarlet dawn. I had a son. I was a father. I felt flooded with joy, as though everything in my life finally meant something.

I was coming home with my wife and our

child. I couldn't believe the happiness. I felt we could face absolutely anything; we'd face it together. It was like a Christmas present from fate; that's how I felt about it anyway. But in another way it was nothing at all, just a moment in a life. It was a radio on a ship a few days before Christmas, among drunks and dreamers, in the darkness. "A broken hallelujah," Leonard Cohen might have said. But maybe that's the best kind of all.